New York City

by Christina Leaf
Illustrated by Diego Vaisberg

BLASTOFF!
MISSIONS

 BELLWETHER MEDIA
MINNEAPOLIS, MN

Blastoff! Missions takes you on a learning adventure! Colorful illustrations and exciting narratives highlight cool facts about our world and beyond. Read the mission goals and follow the narrative to gain knowledge, build reading skills, and have fun!

Traditional Nonfiction

Narrative Nonfiction

Blastoff! Universe

MISSION GOALS ■ ■ ■ ■ ■ ■ ■

> FIND YOUR SIGHT WORDS IN THE BOOK.

> LEARN ABOUT DIFFERENT PERIODS IN NEW YORK CITY'S HISTORY.

> IDENTIFY THREE PEOPLE GROUPS THAT HAVE LIVED IN NEW YORK CITY.

This edition first published in 2024 by Bellwether Media, Inc.

Library of Congress Cataloging-in-Publication Data

Names: Leaf, Christina, author. | Vaisberg, Diego, illustrator.
Title: New York City / by Christina Leaf ; Diego Vaisberg [illustrator].
Description: Minneapolis, MN : Bellwether Media, 2024. | Series: Cities through time | Includes bibliographical references and index. | Audience: Ages 5-8 | Audience: Grades 2-3 | Summary: "Vibrant illustrations accompany information about the history of New York City. The narrative nonfiction text is intended for students in kindergarten through third grade." -- Provided by publisher.
Identifiers: LCCN 2023014278 (print) | LCCN 2023014279 (ebook) | ISBN 9798886873832 (library binding) | ISBN 9798886875218 (paperback) | ISBN 9798886875713 (ebook)
Subjects: LCSH: New York (N.Y.)--History--Juvenile literature.
Classification: LCC F128.33 .L43 2024 (print) | LCC F128.33 (ebook) | DDC 974.7/1--dc23/eng/20230328
LC record available at https://lccn.loc.gov/2023014278
LC ebook record available at https://lccn.loc.gov/2023014279

Editor: Betsy Rathburn   Designer: Andrea Schneider

Printed in the United States of America, North Mankato, MN.

This is **Blastoff Jimmy**! He is here to help you on your mission and share fun facts along the way!

Table of Contents

Welcome to New York!

Look around! New York City, USA, is filled with people and **culture**. How did it become this way? Let's travel through its past to find out. We will move fast. Try to keep up!

► **JIMMY SAYS** ◄
Stories say the Lenape sold Mannahatta for $24. But they likely thought they were sharing the land.

wigwam

The skyscrapers of today's Manhattan are nowhere in sight. Instead, the Lenape's **wigwams** sit among forests and hills.

A Colonial Town

mid-1600s

This new port town of New Amsterdam is busy!

It is part of a Dutch **colony**. Traders from other countries live here, too. The town is becoming **diverse**!

Now the city is New York.
It is under British rule.
It is bigger than ever!

JIMMY SAYS

New York City was the first capital of the United States! It held this title from 1785 to 1790.

More change is coming. People want freedom from Britain. The city will see some battles!

A Growing City

early 1900s

New York City keeps growing! That boat of **immigrants** is landing at Ellis Island. They are looking for new lives. They will build New York into a great city!

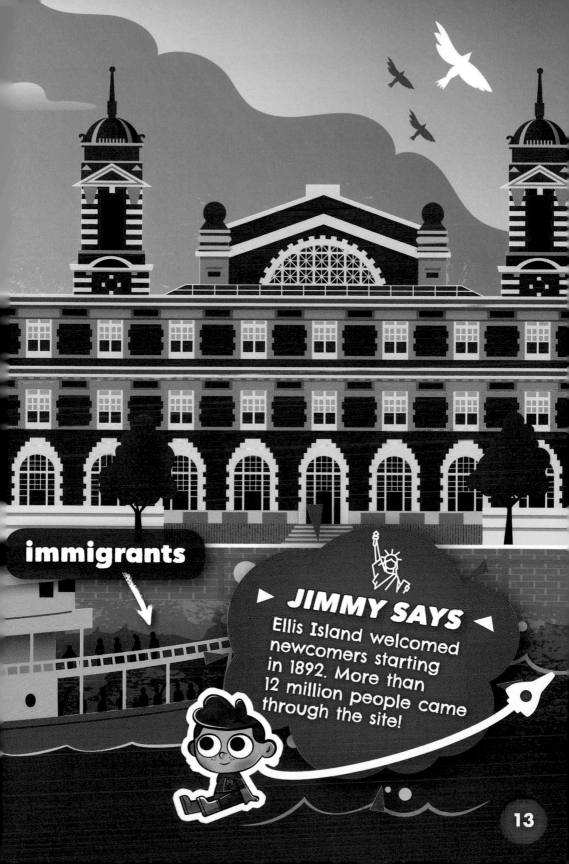

immigrants

► **JIMMY SAYS** ◄
Ellis Island welcomed newcomers starting in 1892. More than 12 million people came through the site!

13

Other changes also bring growth. Uptown, art fills Harlem. African American artists find **inspiration** in their new home!

The new Empire State Building stands tall downtown. Soon, even more skyscrapers will rise around it!

2001

It is a dark time in New York City history. **Terrorists** crashed planes into the World Trade Center.

But the city stands strong. People come together to help each other!

The City Today

today

Stroll through the five **boroughs** to see the city today. All kinds of people live here!

You will hear different languages and smell many **cuisines**. From **bodegas** to skyscrapers, New York City has it all!

We saw just a small part of New York City's history today. But there is still more to come for this great city!

New York City Timeline

pre-1600s: Lenape people live on the island of Mannahatta

1626: Mannahatta, now Manhattan, comes under Dutch control

1664: Britain takes over New Amsterdam and names it New York

1776: The Battle of Fort Washington takes place on Manhattan during the Revolutionary War

1892: Ellis Island begins welcoming immigrants

1931: The Empire State Building is finished while a rich period of art happens in Harlem

2001: Terrorists crash planes into the World Trade Center

New York City, U.S.A.

Glossary

bodegas–small grocery stores, often in cities

boroughs–the five different areas of New York Cit

colony–an area controlled by a faraway country

cuisines–styles of cooking

culture–the beliefs, arts, and ways of life in a pla or society

diverse–made up of people from many different backgrounds

immigrants–people who move to a new country

inspiration–ideas about what to do or create

terrorists–people who use fear to control others

wigwams–homes made of bark or animal furs covering a structure of wooden poles

To Learn More

AT THE LIBRARY

Arrhenius, Ingela P. *My First Book of New York.* Somerville, Mass.: Walker Books, 2019.

Messinger, Carla, with Susan Katz. *When the Shadbush Blooms.* New York, N.Y.: Lee & Low Books, 2020.

Thermes, Jennifer. *Manhattan: Mapping the Story of an Island.* New York, N.Y.: Abrams Books for Young Readers, 2019.

ON THE WEB

FACTSURFER

Factsurfer.com gives you a safe, fun way to find more information.

1. Go to www.factsurfer.com.

2. Enter "New York City" into the search box and click 🔍.

3. Select your book cover to see a list of related content.

BEYOND THE MISSION

> WHAT FACT FROM THE BOOK DID YOU THINK WAS THE MOST INTERESTING?

> WHICH POINT IN NEW YORK CITY HISTORY WOULD YOU LIKE TO VISIT? WHY?

> DRAW A PICTURE OF WHAT YOU THINK NEW YORK CITY WILL LOOK LIKE IN THE FUTURE.

Index